Black Heroes
of the
Wild West

"We need in literature the kind of black men and women all of us know exist in life; who are not afraid to claim our rights as human beings and as Americans."

—*Langston Hughes*

"The Need for Heroes," written in observance of his twentieth year as a contributor to the NAACP magazine *The Crisis*, June 1941.

BLACK·HEROES
of the WILD·WEST

by **Ruth Pelz**

♦

illustrations by **Leandro Della Piana**

FIRST EDITION

OPEN HAND PUBLISHING INC.
Seattle, Washington

Open Hand Publishing Inc.
P.O. Box 22048
Seattle, Washington 98122
(206) 323-3868

Book and cover design by Deb Figen

Library of Congress Card Catalog Number: 89-63500
ISBN: 0-940880-25-3 cloth cover
ISBN: 0-940880-26-1 paperback

First Edition
Printed in the United States of America
95 94 93 92 91 90   7 6 5 4 3 2 1

Table of Contents

Estevan *1*

Jean Baptiste Point Du Sable *7*

George Washington Bush *13*

James Beckwourth *19*

Clara Brown *25*

Biddy Mason *31*

Mifflin Gibbs *37*

Mary Fields *43*

Bill Pickett *49*

Bibliography *53*

Estevan

Born: about 1501 ♦ *Died: 1539*

The year was 1539. A large group of people was walking across the Arizona desert. In the lead was a tall, powerful black man named Estevan. He wore turquoise and gold jewelry and brightly colored feathers. Dozens of little bells tinkled happily as he walked. Two sleek greyhounds trotted beside him, and as many as 300 Indians followed behind.

They all were headed north. They were searching for seven cities, seven wonderful cities that legends had told them about.

Estevan did not live to finish his journey. But this man, who was searching for a legend, became a legend himself. It is not hard to understand why. His life was as full of adventures as any hero you may read about.

These adventures began in 1527. In that year, Estevan, who was born in Africa, was brought to America as a slave. He and his Spanish master were bound for Florida. They were to help explore that area for the King of Spain.

For weeks they marched with 300 other men

through thick jungles and terrible swamps. The weather was hot and steamy. The men had little food. Mosquitoes, poisonous snakes, and deadly diseases were everywhere. In some places Indians attacked the travelers.

Many men died. The others decided to build wooden rafts and float out to sea. They would try to sail to Spanish settlements in Mexico.

They didn't make it. When they were near the present border of Texas and Louisiana, a terrible storm came up. All the rafts were wrecked or lost. Estevan and the other survivors were captured. They were made to work for the Indian tribes nearby.

They remained with their captors for more than five years. Life was so hard that soon only four were left alive, Estevan, his master, and two other Spaniards. They lived with different tribes, but they all thought about how they might join together and escape.

At last they had their chance. Each autumn the tribes gathered to harvest a kind of wild fruit called prickly pears. On the night of the full moon, the four men crept away to a planned meeting place. They were free!

Now the most amazing adventure of all began. Here they were, all alone on the Texas plain. They had no maps, of course, no food, no tools, and no shelter. They hoped to reach the closest Spanish settlement, but they did not even know where it was.

All they had was their experience. In years of living

with the Indians, they had learned much about their way of life. They had learned how to survive. Estevan, who had a special talent for this, had learned several Indian languages. All of this would be very important to the travelers.

Hurrying to go as far as they could before winter began, the men headed west. They soon arrived at a village of friendly Indians. Some members of the village approached them and said, "We have heard that you are medicine men. Will you please try to cure our sick?"

The four travelers knew only a little about healing. Still, they had seen Indian medicine men at work before. They decided they must try. Amazingly, they were able to help many people get well. News of their successes traveled from tribe to tribe. As the men continued their journey, they received a warm welcome from other Indian villages along the way.

In each place, Estevan spoke with the people. He asked them about the lands and villages nearby. He asked about the best trails to follow. He helped the Spanish learn about lands and people that no one other than the native people had ever seen before.

On and on they continued, over deserts and mountains, through green valleys and back into deserts again. They walked for more than a year and more than 1,000 miles! Finally, one day in March, 1536, they found what they had been seeking. They met a group of Spanish soldiers. Their journey had ended!

The four men were welcomed as heroes. Everyone listened in awe as they told of their adventures.

One story was especially exciting. Estevan had heard about seven great cities that lay to the north. "They are beautiful cities," the Indians had said. "They have tall buildings made of stone. They are rich in turquoise, silver, and soft, woven cloth."

Spanish legends told about seven lost cities of great wealth. Perhaps these were the very ones. The Spanish ruler decided to send some people to look for these cities. Estevan would be the guide. He became the first explorer to visit the lands that would become the western United States.

Unfortunately, Estevan died during the journey. The seven cities were never found. But the Zuni Indians of New Mexico still have a legend about the brave black man who entered their village. And schoolchildren around the United States still learn about the African who explored our lands.

Jean Baptiste Pointe Du Sable

Born: 1745 ♦ *Died: 1818*

The storm was a fierce one. Rain poured down from heavy gray clouds. Howling winds screamed across the water and stirred up huge waves. From time to time, bolts of lightning ripped through the sky. The thunder that followed was deafening.

In the middle of it all, a small wooden ship tossed dangerously from side to side. On its deck, two young men struggled to keep the ship afloat. They were Jean Baptiste Pointe Du Sable and his friend, Jacques Clemorgan. "Trim the sails!" yelled Jean. "Help me tie down the ropes!" He could barely be heard over the wind and rain and crashing waves.

Jean's father was an experienced French seaman. He was the owner of this ship. Jean, too, knew much about the sea. He and Jacques had grown up by the water on the island of Haiti. But everything Jean Du Sable knew was not enough to save the ship. The storm was too fierce. The waves were too high. Suddenly, with a mighty crash, the ship rolled over and began to sink.

The men were thrown into the raging sea. After

hours in the rough waters, they finally reached the shore. They had lost everything they owned, but they survived.

When he was well again, Jacques found a job in New Orleans. Things were not so easy for Jean Du Sable. You see, Jacques Clemorgan was white, but his friend was not. Jean's mother was an African slave. In New Orleans, at that time, a black man like Jean might be captured and sold as a slave.

Jean Du Sable had been educated at a Catholic school. Now he turned to the Church for help. A kindly priest took him in. He gave Jean a home and a job in the Catholic mission.

In time Jean was joined by another young man in need. He was a Potawatomi Indian named Choctaw. The Potawatomi's home was far to the north, near the Great Lakes. It was a land of thick forests, grassy plains and cold, clear waters. Hundreds of kinds of wild animals lived there: beaver, marten, otter, buffalo, deer, and many others. Their soft, warm furs made wonderful winter clothing. Trapping the animals and selling their furs became an important business on the frontier. Choctaw had worked in the fur trade for many years. He trapped the wild animals and brought their skins to New Orleans to sell. On this trip, however, he had been cheated of his pay. Like Jean Du Sable, he had no place to turn but to the Church.

The two young men worked together in the mission garden. They shared many hours of conversation. Choctaw told his friend about life on the frontier. "There are no masters there and no slaves," he said. "The land is beautiful and rich." They talked on, until Jean decided that he too must become a fur trader.

He went to his friend Jacques, who became excited about the idea. "I have saved some money from my job," he said. "And I am ready for adventure. You and Choctaw and I can go into business together."

They did. The three young men headed up the Mississippi River in 1765. Choctaw taught Jean and Jacques how to set traps, how to skin the animals they caught, and how to survive in the wilderness. Soon they had a growing business. Jean and Choctaw traveled up the rivers each year in search of furs. Then Jacques took the furs to New Orleans to sell them. He also ran a trading post beside the river.

This went on for several years. Jean Du Sable traveled throughout the Middle West. He learned the skills required on the frontier. He learned the ways of the frontier Indian tribes and got along well with them. He won their respect. He even served as a peacemaker, helping to end fighting among the tribes.

In all his travels, there was one place that Jean Du Sable most wanted to live. It was a grassy plain not far from the most southern point on the Great Lakes. Thick forests stood nearby. Flowing rivers connected the lakes with the Mississippi River. It was a great crossroads, a wonderful place to build a city. It was the place the Indians called "Eschikagou."

Jean Du Sable was determined to live there someday. In time he did. He built the first cabin and the first trading post beside the river. Later he added a stable, a dairy, a workshop, a mill, and a large house that faced the water. Around the buildings were his farms and fields and herds of animals. Jean married a Potawatomi woman named Catherine and brought her to Eschikagou to live. Their children were the first to be born in the new settlement there.

Under Du Sable's leadership, the settlement grew into a busy trading center. Over time it would become one of the largest cities in the whole United States, the city of Chicago, Illinois.

There were dangers and difficulties along the way. During America's war of independence, fighting broke out around the Great Lakes. Sooner or later, everyone was drawn into it—Indians, Americans, English, and French. Jean Du Sable sided with the Americans in their fight against England. He was captured by English soldiers and held prisoner for several months. Then the war ended. The United States had won.

The new government was not always fair to Du Sable and other early settlers. Jean and Catherine were not able to keep their land and their buildings. They retired to a farm in Peoria and lived there quietly in their old age.

Jean Baptiste Pointe Du Sable did not live to see Chicago grow into a great city. He would not recognize the tall buildings that stand where he once made his home. But the city Du Sable started has recognized him. He is honored today as Chicago's first citizen.

George Washington Bush

Born: Between 1779 and 1790 ◆ *Died: 1863*

"**I** bet you can't hit that tree with a snowball!" yelled Rial Bailey Bush to his younger brother.

"Can too!" Henry replied.

"Show me."

Henry Sanford Bush took extra care to pack his snowball hard and tight. His bare hands were already red from the cold, but this was important. He looked at the tree again. He raised his arm, pulled it back, and let go. The snowball made a satisfying WHACK! against the tree trunk.

Just then the boys' older brothers called them. "Come on," they yelled. "Father says we can begin traveling again. Come and help."

The boys ran back to camp. There all the families were hurrying to get ready. They loaded their wagons and hitched up the teams of oxen. Then, one by one, the slow and heavy animals began to pull the wagons down the trail. The last part of the trip had begun!

For months now, the families had been traveling across the great Oregon Trail. They had walked nearly 2,000 miles across the endless grasslands of the Great

Plains and over the Rocky Mountains. Back and forth across countless rivers. There were no roads or bridges to make the trip easier. There were no stores or cities, no houses or hospitals along the way. Some days no food or water could be found. Several people had died of accidents or disease. The others were just tired!

It was late in the year before they arrived in the Blue Mountains—too late. They had been trapped in a snowstorm and had to wait till the weather improved. Now, finally, they were moving again. They were climbing the last rugged stretch of these mountains, heading west.

Suddenly someone shouted, "There it is!" Below them lay the wide and sparkling waters of the Columbia River. It was the sight they had all traveled so far to see. Excited, Isabelle Bush called her boys. "Look!" she said happily. "It's the mighty river your father has told you about. The one that flows through the good lands of Oregon all the way to the Pacific Ocean. Just imagine! The end of our journey is finally near!"

The boys ran off to look for their father. They found him talking with several other men. George Washington Bush was one of the most respected members of the wagon train. He was the only one who had been West before. He had worked for a fur trading company when he was a young man. Now all the travelers depended on his knowledge and advice.

"There is hard country ahead of us," said Mr. Bush.

"For days now, there will be no trees and little food. Anything you see that's as big as a blackbird, shoot it and eat it!"

As the travelers continued their journey, George Washington Bush had other worries beside food. He shared his worries with his friend John Minto. He said, "In Missouri I was a wealthy man. I had a big farm and a large herd of cattle. But life in Missouri is not easy for a man with dark skin, not even a wealthy man with an educated white wife like Isabelle. We hoped that far away, on the frontier, we might finally live in peace.

"Now, we have come all this way, but we don't know what we'll find. We don't know if I, as a black man, will be welcome in Oregon. If the settlers there do not treat us well, we may have to move on.

Many miles later, the news came. The Oregon settlers had just voted that no blacks would be allowed to settle nearby. The travelers were upset and angry. George and Isabelle Bush had helped families in need all through the trip. They were respected. They were friends.

"Listen," the travelers said, "American settlers control only the area south of the Columbia River. North of the river, English traders with the Hudson's Bay Company are in control. The company has said it wants no families to settle on their land, but we must try."

It was decided. Four other families and two single

men, all white, chose to join George and Isabelle Bush. They all headed north of the Columbia River and settled near Puget Sound. They were the first United States citizens to settle there.

The year was 1845. Both the United States and England wanted the lands around Puget Sound. Which nation would get them? At that time, nobody knew. The next year, an agreement was reached. The lands would belong to the United States. Some people feel this might not have happened if the Bush family and their friends had not been living there. Their settlement helped give the United States a stronger claim.

Within a few years, George Washington Bush and his family were raising large herds of cattle and crops of corn, beans, pumpkins, potatoes, and wheat. They built a mill on the river to grind wheat into flour. They built a sawmill to cut logs into boards.

By then, many more settlers had arrived. George Washington Bush continued to help his neighbors. He got along well with the Indians nearby. People in need knew that they could turn to him for gifts of seed and food.

But, the Bush family still had problems. New laws said that only white settlers could claim the land. Would George and Isabelle Bush lose the farm they had worked so hard to build? Their neighbors said "NO!" They went to the new government of the Washington Territory and asked for help. In 1855 a special law was passed to allow the Bush family to keep their land. (Later, George and Isabelle's son, William Owen Bush, would be elected a senator in the Territory's government.)

Today George Washington Bush is known as one of the founders of Washington State. The area where he lived is still named for him. It is called Bush Prairie. It is a fitting way to remember a very important citizen.

James Beckwourth

Born: 1798 ♦ *Died: 1866*

Jim Beckwourth crouched behind a thick shrub and peered into the forest. There it was! Quickly and silently he raised his rifle, aimed, and pulled the trigger. The explosion echoed from the huge trees around him. Jim rushed forward. A big buck deer lay dead in the undergrowth.

A sound of brushing leaves attracted Jim's attention. He turned his head and saw his new friend, an Indian about his own age, coming toward him. "Good shot," the young man signaled to him, moving his hands. "Good food. You and your friends will not go hungry."

Young Jim Beckwourth felt proud. This was his first trip into the wilderness and already he had learned so much. He had learned to track animals and to find his own way through the great forests. He was becoming a good hunter. He had provided good meals for the traders who were making this trip. Sometimes Jim went hunting with young men from the Indian villages along the way. He learned a lot from them—about tracking and hunting, about Indian life and languages.

It was all so different from his life in St. Louis! There in the city, Jim had been learning to be a blacksmith. He stood all day over a hot fire, making horseshoes, tools, and other metal objects. But Jim was too restless for that kind of work. He wanted to travel. He wanted to test himself.

Beyond St. Louis stood the great frontier. There were no towns or cities for a thousand miles—just thick forests, high mountains, vast deserts. It was the home of countless Indian tribes, but few other people, black or white, had visited it. Jim Beckwourth wanted to try.

Life on the frontier wasn't for everyone. It was rough and uncomfortable and dangerous. But it was full of challenges and adventures, and that suited young Jim Beckwourth just fine. After his first trip, Jim went back again and again. He became one of the best-known trappers of the Rocky Mountain Fur Company.

He had more adventures than most people even dreamed about. Once, he said, he was charged by a wounded buffalo and nearly killed. On one early trip, he and a companion almost starved to death. Luckily, a band of Kansas Indians found them and cared for them just in time. Another time Jim was attacked by Indians from a different tribe. He was badly wounded. Jim's friend thought he had died, but he lived through it.

James Beckwourth lived through encounters with

bears and other wild animals. He lived through freezing winters in the mountains and dangerous river crossings in the spring. He survived years of traveling through the wilderness completely alone.

He also survived many battles between enemy Indian tribes. Jim Beckwourth fought in those battles as fearlessly as any member of the tribe. In fact, he even became an Indian chief! This is how it happened. Jim was captured by members of the Crow tribe. One of the Crow women looked at Jim and believed he was her long-lost son. Jim didn't argue. It seemed better to go along with the idea.

Jim stayed with the Crow tribe for several years. He was accepted by the Indians as one of their own. He married the chief's daughter and became a famous Crow warrior. Because of his leadership skills, he was chosen as chief.

But Jim remained restless. He left the Crows and returned to visit his family in St. Louis. There he was hired by the United States Army. It was common for fur traders to work as army scouts. Their skills at traveling through the wilderness and their understanding of Indian cultures made them useful. Black, white, and Indian trappers all filled this role.

Jim was a successful scout, but he didn't like it. He decided to go into business for himself. He started his own trading posts in different locations around the West.

One of his posts was in California, near the gold mines. While he was there, Jim decided to go looking for gold himself. On one of his trips into the mountains he made a very important discovery.

He had climbed high that day. He stood on a peak and looked at the mountains around him. They were rough and dangerous. Many travelers had died trying to cross through on their way to the gold fields.

How many times Jim had stood on a peak like this, looking for a way through the rough lands ahead! Now his experienced eye was drawn to an area of lower, gentler hills. Could that be a pass through the mountains? Would it be a better route to California? Jim decided to find out.

On his next trip, Jim went exploring. He did find a pass. He led the first group of settlers across it. Jim Beckwourth had successfully opened an important path for westward travelers. Today that pass, a nearby mountain peak, a valley, and a town in Nevada all have his name. This great adventurer, who thrived on the dangers of the Wild West, made life safer for those who came after him.

Clara Brown

Born: 1803 ♦ *Died: 1885*

"**S**hoo!" said the old woman. "Get out of here!" A neighbor's pig had gotten into her garden again. Aunt Clara Brown shook her broom, and the fat, dirty pig waddled away. The animal trotted past a few tiny wooden houses and disappeared. In another yard, chickens were pecking and clucking about, the sound of barking dogs could be heard.

Aunt Clara sighed. They called this place Central City, but it was not much of a city at all. A few rows of small houses clung to the side of a steep hill. Down below, on Main Street, were the town's few businesses. Most of them were saloons.

Clara looked down the dirt street. After a rain, that street was nothing but mud. Aunt Clara and the other women lifted up their long skirts and walked with care.

Of course, there weren't many women in Central City then. The rough Colorado mining towns were mostly full of men. These men spent their days in the mountains, looking for gold and silver or working in the mines. They came to town to eat and drink and gamble. Often fights started. Mining towns were some of the wildest places in the Wild West.

Aunt Clara was more than 60 years old, but she worked harder than a woman half her age. She kept busy doing the work that men didn't want to do. She opened a laundry. She washed the miners' clothes. She worked as a nurse. She started the first Sunday school. Pretty soon everyone in town knew her as someone who would lend a helping hand.

Clara Brown knew how important help could be. There had been many times when she could have used some help herself. As she went back to her washing, she thought about the experiences that had brought her here.

Memories of the early days were painful. She had been born a slave, in Virginia, in 1803. Slaves didn't have anything, she thought sadly. They didn't even have their families. One by one, Clara's husband and children had been taken from her and sold. Clara herself was sold many times before she was able to buy her freedom. Someday she was going to find her family and buy their freedom too. That was the dream that brought her to Central City.

How she remembered those early stories of the gold in California and later in Colorado! For blacks and whites alike, the West seemed a land of promise. Aunt Clara Brown began to think of going west herself. Finally she had her chance. She found a group of miners who would hire her as a cook. At the age of 59, she left Missouri in a wagon train.

Two months later, she arrived in Denver. There she helped start a Sunday school. But she knew that the greatest opportunities lay in the mining towns. Central City was one of the busiest, and Clara Brown decided to settle there.

Aunt Clara had done well. She made quite a bit of money. She managed to save $10,000 from the earnings of her laundry business along with investments she had made in mining shares. As she hung up the clothes to dry, Clara dreamed again of what she would do with all that money. She would find her family. She would buy a covered wagon and bring them all to Central City. She would build a fine house with a big yard.

Her dreams were interrupted by a noise in the street. "Oh dear," thought Clara. "Not that pig again!" She went out to look.

It was a neighbor running excitedly down the street.

"Mrs. Brown!" he cried. "The War Between the States is over. The Union has won!" The man continued down the street, sharing his news with everyone he met.

Clara Brown felt a shiver of excitement. Her hands were trembling. "Now!" she said to herself. "Now I can begin."

Over the next few years, she searched for her family in every way she could. She found 34 distant relatives. She helped them and many other African Americans to come west in wagon trains. But she never found her husband or her children.

The people of Central City became her family. She never refused help to a person in need, black or white. Wealthy and well-respected, Clara Brown was known as one of the town's leading citizens. At the very end of her life, this determined woman received one last wonderful surprise. One of her daughters finally found her. A part of her dream had at last come true.

Biddy Mason

Born: about 1820 ♦ *Died: 1891*

"**M**ama, I'm tired," said the little girl. "It's hot and I'm tired of walking. Why can't we stop now? Why can't we stay where we are?"

"Hush now," said Biddy, comforting her daughter. "I know you're tired. I've had enough of traveling myself, more than enough. But it isn't my choice, child. It's Mr. Robert Smith says if we're walking or staying. And Mr. Smith is a traveling kind of man. You get up in the wagon with your sister for a while."

Sometimes it seemed they would never stop traveling. First there had been the long trip to Utah. All day Biddy had walked along behind the wagons, tending the cattle. For months they walked, getting farther and farther from Mississippi. It was a hard trip, especially for the children. But what could Biddy do? She was born a slave. She was a slave today. Her master told her to walk across the plains and she did it.

They had stayed in Utah only one year. Then word came of a new settlement in Southern California. Robert Smith decided to go. Again the wagons were packed. Again they began the long days of walking.

Biddy had plenty of time for thinking along the way. What she mostly thought about was freedom. As a child she had never known a black person who wasn't a slave. Oh, she heard about them, about the ones who escaped to the North. But it was all so hard to imagine!

Then came the trip west. Things were different here. She had seen families, *black families,* traveling west with their own wagons! Just think of it! They planned to find their own land, start their own farms, or find work in the towns. Biddy had thought about them for days.

Then there was Salt Lake City. Mormon families had come there from all over the country. Some came from the South and brought slaves with them. Many families came from the northern states, though, where slavery wasn't allowed. It was different, all right. It got you thinking.

Biddy looked down at her bare feet. They were tired and sore and covered with dust. "These feet walked every mile from Mississippi," she thought. "And they remember every step. They have walked for Mr. Smith and his family. They have walked after his crops and his wagons and his cattle. But someday they are going to walk for me. Some day these feet will walk me to freedom! I'm sure of it."

A few days later, the tired travelers arrived at San Bernardino, California. It was a lovely place. It was their new home.

There were many reasons to enjoy living in California in 1852. The climate was pleasant. The land was good. The air was fresh and warm. Cities were booming. Everywhere there was a sense of promise and excitement.

The most important thing for Biddy was the promise of freedom. She had heard people talking. The new state of California did not permit slavery, they said. By law all people here were free. Biddy looked again at her dusty traveling feet. "Soon," she said to herself, "soon."

Three years passed. Life was pretty good, but Mr. Smith must have loved traveling. Even this beautiful settlement could not hold him. He decided to move again, this time to Texas. The wagons were loaded and made ready to go.

Biddy knew she had to act. As soon as the wagons

left San Bernardino, she began looking for an opportunity. She found one. Somehow she sent word to the sheriff in Los Angeles. He stopped the wagons before they left California.

"I hear you have slaves in your party," said the sheriff. "I suppose you know that's against the law. Is it true?"

Biddy came forward. In all her life this was the first time she had ever spoke to a white sheriff. Still her voice was strong. "It is true," she said. "Mr. Smith is taking us to Texas and we don't want to go."

That statement led to the most important slavery trial in Southern California. Biddy and another slave woman and the their children were taken to court. Biddy spoke to the judge, and once again, her words were strong and clear: "I want to stay in California. I want to be free."

The judge sided with Biddy. He scolded Mr. Smith for breaking the law. He gave all the slaves their freedom.

Biddy gathered up her children and said, "We are moving once more, but it won't be very far. We are going to Los Angeles, and this time," she said, looking at her tired feet, "I am walking for me!"

She started her new life by taking as her full name, Biddy Mason. She went to work as a nurse and a housekeeper. Before long she saved enough to buy a house. Soon she bought other property too. Biddy

Mason was a good businesswoman. She became one of the wealthiest blacks in Los Angeles.

She shared that wealth with others. She gave land to build schools and hospitals and nursing homes. She supported the education of black children and helped people in need. Biddy Mason had come a long way from that slave's cabin in Mississippi. She still remembered the walking. And she made sure she helped others along their way.

Mifflin Gibbs

Born: 1823 ♦ *Died: 1903*

Mifflin Gibbs was only twelve years old, but he was already earning a living. He had been working for four years—ever since his father died. He took care of rich people's horses. It was one job a free black child in Philadelphia could do.

Today Mifflin was sitting on a train, speeding out of Philadelphia, heading south. Beside him sat Sidney Fisher, the man he worked for. They were off to visit Mr. Fisher's plantation in Maryland.

Through the windows of the train, Mifflin saw something he had never seen before. There were hundreds of dark-skinned people working in the fields, working hard, looking tired and sad. They did not talk with each other or even look up. They were working in fear of a man who stood over them, a man with a gun and a whip. It was horrible!

"Who are they?" Mifflin whispered, almost afraid to speak.

"Those are slaves," Mr. Fisher replied. "We live in Pennsylvania, a free state. No slavery is allowed. But Maryland is different. It is like the rest of the South."

Mifflin Gibbs never forgot that moment. His mother had talked to him about slavery. He knew it was wrong. But he never really *understood* before. He resolved, right then, to fight against slavery however he could.

As a teenager, Mifflin studied carpentry. He soon was putting up buildings himself. At night he read and studied. In keeping with his childhood promise, he began to work and speak and write against slavery.

When he was still a young man, the great black leader, Frederick Douglass, asked Mifflin to join him. They would tour New York State, giving talks against slavery.

Mifflin agreed, but the tour was a hard one. What they were saying was not popular and was not well-received.

Mifflin began to pay attention to the stories he heard about California. They were stories of gold! The first discovery had been made in 1849. After that the news spread like wildfire. Soon nearly everyone had a story to tell.

"I heard about a schoolteacher who made a fortune."

"I know a man who made two thousand dollars in a single day!"

"They say there are gold nuggets as big as your hand!"

"One miner was born a slave and now is richer than his master. He is going to buy all of his family their freedom!"

"Anyone can go to California and grow rich!"

Mifflin Gibbs decided to try. He was one of perhaps 2,000 African Americans who joined the gold rush to California.

There were many ways to make money in California in those days. Some people headed for the mountains. They searched through the gravel in rivers and streams. This is where the first gold was found. Some of the miners grew rich indeed. They came down from the mountains with money to spend! Other people went to work selling things to the miners.

Mifflin Gibbs was one of these. He started as a shoeshiner, outside a San Francisco hotel. San Francisco was an exciting place to be in those days. Every day ships and people arrived from all over the world. The city grew faster than anything anyone had seen. Wealthy miners built beautiful houses and fabulous hotels. From the waterfront to the city's steep hillsides, everywhere there was building going on. But construction work was not open to blacks, not even to a skilled carpenter like Mifflin Gibbs.

Mifflin was not a man to become discouraged. He shined shoes and saved money. Before long he became a shoe-store owner. He would own other stores before his life was through. Still, he never lost his interest in politics.

Although California was a free state, many of the new state laws were unfair to African Americans.

Once again Mifflin Gibbs spoke out. He made speeches. He talked to state government leaders. He wrote about important issues. In 1855 he helped to start a newspaper, the first black-owned paper in the state. But despite the hard work of Mifflin Gibbs and others, prejudice against black Californians continued to grow.

In 1858 there was news of another gold strike. This one was in Canada. Perhaps there a talented black man could find a better life. Mifflin joined another gold rush. He traveled to the Fraser River Valley, just north of the United States border. There, he opened another store, married a woman from the United States, and once again got involved in politics. By 1866 he was elected to the local government.

Another man would have been happy to stay there, enjoying his wealth and his position in the community. But not Councilman Gibbs. Things had changed a lot in the United States by then, and Mifflin wanted to go home. The Civil War had been fought and won. Slavery had ended. There were opportunities for African Americans that had never existed before.

Mifflin Gibbs decided to move to Arkansas and study law. In 1873 he was elected to be a judge. In later years, the President of the United States appointed him to other government posts.

The little boy from Philadelphia was convinced he could succeed, and he did—as a businessman, a government leader, and a defender of people's rights. He faced many challenges, but he never lost his confidence. He achieved what he set out to do and more!

Mary Fields

Born: ? ♦ *Died: 1914*

Mary Fields squinted and pulled her coat up as high as she could. She tried to protect her face from the biting wind. Winters in Montana were cold enough to turn her bones to ice, she thought. But she would not think of leaving, not for one minute. Certainly she never wanted to return to the slave's cabin in Tennessee where she was born! Besides, she was needed here. The nuns at Saint Peter's Mission School depended on her. Mary tended their cows and chickens and hauled their supplies.

Take this trip, for example. Who else would have hitched up the horses and driven the wagon over the snow-covered plains? Who else would have loaded the heavy boxes and bundles? Nothing would stop her when a trip had to be made - not rain or snow or fierce winter winds. Not the evening's darkness that closed in around her now.

The last fading light was reflected weakly by the snow. In the distance, all was shadow. Not a single light, not a single house or building could be seen. Mary Fields was all alone in the vast darkness.

A gust of wind whistled across the plain. Some of the shadows appeared to shift or move. Without thinking, Mary reached over to be sure that her rifle was still at her side, ready to use. She felt the handle of her revolver under her coat. She cracked the horse's reins, urging them on.

Suddenly a high, moaning sound broke the silence. Mary felt a shiver raise the hair on her neck. The horse seemed to shiver too, and grew nervous. The first sound was joined by another. And another. The chilling, lonely howl grew louder. It seemed to surround them on all sides. "Wolves!" thought Mary.

The horses panicked. They jerked forward, racing out of control, trying to break free. The wagon lurched wildly along the rough and frozen trail. Before she knew what was happening, the wagon had tipped over. Mary and her bundles were spilled out onto the snow.

"What a mess!" thought Mary. "I can't take care of this in the dark. I'll be stuck here until morning." She gathered up her rifle and shook off the snow. She listened. The howls had faded away. But Mary could sense that the wolves were still around her. Her guns at the ready, she prepared herself to face the long night alone.

Mary Fields lived through that night and through many other adventures. She was a strong woman. There was no doubt about it. She was as big and powerful as some men are, and she was quick to lose her temper. She was not about to let anyone take advantage of her.

Once, at St. Peter's, someone had tried to bully her. He was a man who had been hired to do some heavy work around the mission. He and Mary got into a fight. They both drew their guns – and used them.

A Catholic school for Indian girls was no place for shoot-outs. Some people complained about Mary's behavior. Finally, Bishop Brondel, the local church leader, ordered Mary to leave the school.

The nuns were sad to see her go. They helped her start a restaurant in the nearby mining town of Cascade. But Mary was not a good businesswoman. The restaurant failed. So the nuns found her another job, one more suited to her skills. Mary would be responsible for delivering the mission's mail. From that day, she met every train that arrived in town. She gathered the items that came for St. Peter's and carried them out to the school. If the weather was too bad for her horses, she carried the mail on her back. She earned the nickname "Stagecoach Mary."

When she was about 70 years old, Mary Fields finally retired. She settled into life in the town. She ran a laundry service. She grew flowers and attended all the town's baseball games, which she loved. And she spent quite a bit of time in the saloon, smoking cigars and drinking with the men.

One day, they say, a man refused to pay his laundry bill. Mary followed him out into the street, punched him hard, and knocked him down. Then she walked calmly back to her friends in the saloon. "I guess that settles his bill, all right," she said.

By the time she died in 1914, Mary Fields was well-known and respected by the people of her town. She was missed by the many friends with whom she had shared her stories.

The Wild West produced many colorful and remarkable men and women. Mary Fields was certainly one of them. She was one of many African Americans who were heroes and leaders in this important part of our nation's history.

Bill Pickett

Born: 1870 ? ♦ *Died: 1932*

The crowd had been waiting for this moment. A huge, angry bull had just been set loose in the rodeo ring. It was tamping and snorting and looking mean. Clouds of dust swirled up as the powerful animal paced and turned.

Then another gate opened. A wiry, tough-looking dark-skinned man rode through the gate. "It's him!" people said excitedly. "It's Bill Pickett."

The man turned for a moment and smiled at the audience. He adjusted his broad-brimmed cowboy hat. Then he leaned down close to the sleek, shining neck of his horse. He was ready!

Bill shouted and charged after the bull. In an instant, he leapt from his horse, flew through the air, and grabbed the bull by its horns. The angry animal bellowed and bucked and tried to break free.

Bill Pickett was not a big man, but he was strong. He dug his boot heels into the ground and pulled with all his might. He twisted and pulled until he forced the bull's nose into the air. One of the horns hooked into the ground, and the bull flipped over. Bill Pickett had wrestled the animal to the ground with his bare hands. That was called "bulldogging."

The crowd cheered, but they were waiting for more. The excitement grew. Would Pickett perform his most famous rodeo trick? He did. He bit into the bull's big lip and raised his hands into the air. Holding the bull with his teeth, Pickett rolled and dragged the animal to a stop. The crowd went wild!

Bill Pickett, they said, had invented the sport of bulldogging, and no one did it better. A few of the West's most famous cowboys had worked with him; Tom Mix and Will Rogers were two of them. They traveled with Bill Pickett as part of the 101 Ranch show. They had lots of adventures. Once, in New York City, a bull escaped and ran up into the seating area. Bill Pickett and another cowboy rode their horses up the steps and herded the animal back into the ring. In Mexico City, in 1908, Bill rode a bull for over five minutes to win a bet. It's a wonder he lived through that one!

Bill Pickett was one of the most famous rodeo riders of all time. He was not just a performer, though. He was a real, working cowboy. Zack Miller, owner of the 101 Ranch, once called him "the greatest sweat-and-dirt cowboy that ever was."

There was plenty of sweat and dirt in a cowboy's life, especially at round-up time. For months the cattle roamed freely around the huge 101 Ranch. They grazed on wild shrubs and grasses and grew fat. In early spring, Bill and the other cowboys rode out to find them.

Breakfast was cooked early over an open fire. Then the men saddled their horses. They split up and rode out across the Oklahoma prairie. The round-up had begun. This morning Bill and his favorite horse, Spradly, headed west. Before long Bill spotted a cow and its calf. The cattle heard him and started to run. But Bill's horse was much faster. Skillfully the cowboy circled around the animals. He closed in, shouting, until the cattle began to move in the direction he wanted them to go.

All day Bill and the other cowboys repeated this process. Hundreds of cattle soon were moving toward the roundup. By midday the men and horses were tired, sweaty, and covered with dust. The cowboys returned to camp, had lunch, saddled fresh horses, and rode out again. They kept working until every possible bull, cow, and calf had been found.

Then the cowboys surrounded the moving cattle. They yelled and waved their hats at the animals and chased after them. It was a noisy, dirty, tiring job. The cattle were mooing and bawling and bleating. Horses galloped back and forth. Dust was kicked up everywhere. Finally the cattle had been formed into a more or less orderly herd. The cowboys rode along beside them. Any cattle that tried to turn off were quickly chased back to the herd again.

In the early days, cowboys had to walk their cattle for hundreds of miles to get to the nearest market towns. Black, white and Mexican cowboys worked together on these long cattle drives. They herded cattle by day and stretched out on blankets at night under the open sky.

Rodeo sports grew out of the skills that cowboys needed every day. Roping, riding, and taming wild animals were all part of the cowboy's job. Nat Love, one of the most famous cowboys, was known for winning three rodeo contests on the same day!

All these skills involved a certain amount of danger. In his lifetime, Bill Pickett broke most of the bones in his body! But he kept on working with ranch animals until he was more than 60 years old. Then one day Bill was trying to rope a wild horse. The animal kicked him in the head, and the great cowboy died. It was 1932.

In 1971 Bill Pickett became the first black to be voted into the Cowboy Hall of Fame in Oklahoma City. Later he received another honor. A statue of the famous bulldogger was put up in Fort Worth, Texas. It stands at the Cowtown Coliseum, where rodeos are held today.

Bibliography

Further Readings for Children and Adults

JUVENILE LITERATURE (High School and below)

Anderson, LaVere. *Saddles and Sabers*. Champaign, IL: Garrard, 1975.

Burt, Olive. *Negroes in the Early West*. New York: Julian Messner, 1969.

Cortesi, Lawrence. *Jean du Sable: Father of Chicago*. New York: Chilton Book Co., 1972.

Durham, Philip, and Everett L. Jones. *The Adventures of the Negro Cowboys*. New York: Dodd Mead, 1966.

Felton, Harold W. *Jim Beckwourth, Mountain Man*. New York: Dodd Mead Co., 1966.

Hancock, Sibyl. *Bill Pickett: First Black Rodeo Star*. New York: Harcourt Brace Jovanovich, Inc., 1977.

Hughes, Langston. *Famous Negro Heroes of America*. New York: Dodd, Mead Co., 1965.

Katz, William Loren. *Black People Who Made the Old West*. New York: Thomas Y. Crowell, 1977.

Parish, Helen Rand. *Estevanico*. New York: Viking, 1974.

Place, Marian T. *Mountain Man: The Life of Jim Beckwourth*. New York: Thomas Crowell, 1970.

Rollings, Charlemae Hill. *They Showed the Way, Forty American Negro Leaders*. New York: Thomas Crowell, 1964.

Stewart, Paul W. and Yvonne Ponce Wallace. *Black Cowboys*. Black American West Museum and Heritage Center, 1986.

Terrell, John Upton. *Estevanico the Black*. Los Angeles: Westernlore Press, 1968.

ADULT BOOKS

Bonner, T. D. *The Life and Adventures of James P. Beckwourth.* New York: Arno Press, 1969.

Bontemps, Arna, and Jack Conroy. *Anyplace but Here.* New York: Hill and Wang, 1966.

Gibbs, Mifflin. *Shadow and Light.* New York: Arno Press, 1968.

Hanes, Bailey. *Bill Pickett, Bulldogger: The Biography of a Black Cowboy.* Norman: University of Oklahoma Press, 1977.

Katz, William Loren. *Black Indians.* New York: Atheneum, 1986.

Katz, William Loren. *The Black West.* Seattle: Open Hand Publishing, 1987.

Lapp, Rudolph. *Blacks in Gold Rush California.* New Haven: Yale University Press, 1977.

Love, Nat. *The Life and Adventures of Nat Love, Better Known in the Cattle Country as "Deadwood Dick," by Himself.* Baltimore: Black Classic Press, 1988.

Porter, Kenneth Wiggins. *The Negro on the American Frontier.* New York: Arno, 1971.

Savage, W. Sherman. *Blacks in the West.* Westport: Greenwood Press, 1976.

Other Books for Young Readers from Open Hand Publishing Inc.

Nightfeathers
by Sundaira Morninghouse, illustrations by Jody Kim. Fanciful Mother Goose-like rhymes with images drawn from the African-American experience.
32 pages   ISBN: 0-940880-27-X   **$8.95** cloth cover
            ISBN: 0-940880-28-8   **$4.95** paperback

"T" is for "Terrific"/"T" es por "Terrífico"
(English/Spanish)
by Mahji Hall
A bilingual alphabet book. Words have been carefully chosen and illustrated from 10 year old Mahji's perspective.
32 pages   ISBN: 0-940880-21-0   **$8.95** cloth cover
            ISBN: 0-940880-22-9   **$3.95** paperback

The Little Bitty Snake
(English/Spanish and English/Japanese)
by Jorma Rodieck
A fanciful story written and illustrated by a nine year old about the journey of a snake to an island and its encounter with an ant. Ronnie Krauss, producer of **Reading Rainbow** says, "an exceptional book . . . full of whimsy, yet full of truth. Has the creative touch of a child, but a command of storytelling that is quite sophisticated."
24 pages   ISBN: 0-940880-03-2   **$4.00** paperback
            (English/Spanish)
            ISBN: 0-940880-07-5   **$4.00** paperback
            (English/Japanese)

See "*BOOK ORDER FORM*" on reverse.

BOOK ORDER FORM

	PAPER	CLOTH	QUANTITY	TOTAL
Nightfeathers	4.95	8.95		
"T" is for "Terrific"	3.95	8.95		
Black Heroes of the Wild West	5.95	9.95		
The Little Bitty Snake (English/Spanish) (English/Japanese)	4.00 4.00			
Postage and Handling ($2.00 for first book, 50¢ for each additional book)				
TOTAL				

Send books to:

NAME
ADDRESS
CITY/STATE/ZIP
PHONE

Make checks payable and send with the order to:

Open Hand Publishing Inc.
P.O. Box 22048
Seattle, Washington 98122
(206) 323-3868

RUTH PELZ has a longstanding interest in uncovering the hidden histories of women and working people as well as ethnic and racial groups in our society. She has learned from personal experience that history is meaningful only if we see ourselves as taking part in it.

This is her fifth book, three of which include biographies to inspire young readers. A resident of Seattle, she has taught in the Seattle Public Schools and at the University of Washington College of Education. She is a writer, editor and curriculum consultant to several publishers, non-profit organizations and government agencies.

LEANDRO DELLA PIANA began his career as a free lance artist apprenticing in the creation of public sculpture in his native city of Boston. This is his first book. Currently he lives in Salt Lake City where he creates theatre sets and works with *Lallapalooza,* an organization that brings children and artists together in a workshop environment. As a teacher his commitment is to motivate young people to explore and understand cultural diversity.

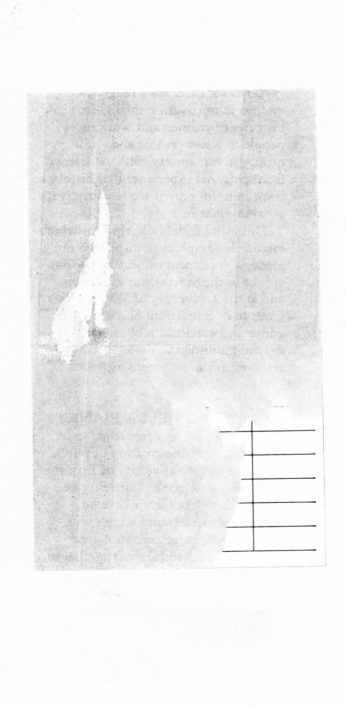